HOW TO RAISE AND TRAIN PET GERBILS

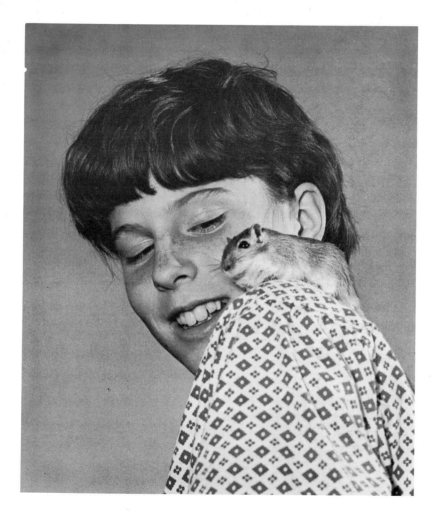

by D. G. Robinson, Jr.

Photographs by the Author

Dedication

This book is dedicated to my wife and children, for their appreciation of my work with gerbils and for their love of animals in general.

Acknowledgments

The author is grateful to Dr. Victor Schwentker for reviewing the manuscript before publication.

Useful information and assistance was also provided by Tumblebrook Farm, Inc.; Creative Playthings, Inc.; Dr. Floyd Leaders of Rodent Ranch; Mr. Russell Roberts of Windy Acres Farm; Mr. J. A. Delfino of Delwood Farms; the Institute of Laboratory Animal Resources; the U.S. Department of the Interior; the National Institutes of Health; and the U.S. Public Health Service.

ISBN 0-87666-195-9

©1967 by TFH PUBLICATIONS, INC.   P.O.Box 27,   Neptune City, N.J. 07753

Distributed in the U.S.A. by T.F.H. Publications, Inc., 211 West Sylvania Avenue, P.O. Box 27, Neptune City, N.J. 07753; in England by T.F.H. (Gt. Britain) Ltd., 13 Nutley Lane, Reigate, Surrey; in Canada to the book store and library trade by Clarke, Irwin & Company, Clarwin House, 791 St. Clair Avenue West, Toronto 10, Ontario; in Canada to the pet trade by Rolf C. Hagen Ltd., 3225 Sartelon Street, Montreal 382, Quebec; in Southeast Asia by Y.W. Ong, 9 Lorong 36 Geylang, Singapore 14; in Australia and the south Pacific by Pet Imports Pty. Ltd., P.O. Box 149, Brookvale 2100, N.S.W., Australia. Published by T.F.H. Publications, Inc. Ltd., The British Crown Colony of Hong Kong.

Contents

A two-month-old gerbil not only has a good sense of balance, but has already reached almost two ounces in weight.

A plastic box with a screened top provides an ideal way for young gerbils and young children to become acquainted. This is a temporary home only, for plastic containers should not be exposed to direct sunlight or the gerbils might be harmed by the heat.

1. Meet the Gerbil

Gerbils are relatively new as pets. For this reason you may be called upon frequently to answer the question, "What's a gerbil?"

With luck, you may find *gerbil* listed in your home dictionary or encyclopedia. The word is pronounced *JUR-bil* and comes from the Latin *gerbillus*, meaning "little jerboa." Probably your reference book will briefly define the gerbil as a "jerboa-like animal." Looking up *jerboa*, you may learn that this is a jumping desert rodent found in Asia and Africa. But this isn't much help, since neither the gerbil nor the jerboa is a native of the Western Hemisphere.

GERBILS IN THE WILD

Gerbils are the typical small mammals found in remote, arid regions of Asia, Africa, and Eastern Europe. They are similar to jumping rodents such as jerboas and "kangaroo rats," but their size, body extremities, and jumping motions are not so exaggerated. They are said to be one of the most graceful small rodents in their movements.

Little is known of the gerbil's life in the wild, where they are called desert rats, sand rats, or jirds. Like hamsters, they are burrowing animals which live far from sources of water. They eat seeds, grains, grasses, roots, and plants found in their desert environment.

Apparently gerbils are active during the day and to some extent at night. They live in colonies and have some close social contact. Their home is a tunnel, 6 to 8 feet long. It has several entrances, extends several feet underground, and usually has branch tunnels at different levels. Various

Pet gerbils are often "smuggled" into school in a boy's pocket.

They possess an unusual abdominal gland that could be useful in studying human hormone actions.

Some experiments have shown that gerbils may be of importance in cancer research.

Studies involving blood composition, body cells, parasitic diseases, and virus infections may also prove significant.

. . . His mind made up, he at last dares to jump down, landing on his forefeet. Note the position of his tail.

In psychology and in behavioral research, gerbils are superior to white rats in some tests, and their docile nature has led to their use in treating some emotionally disturbed children.

There are indications that the gerbil's importance in research may rival that of the hamster in the future. These scientific studies may well lead to discoveries that could benefit mankind and his domestic animals.

Young gerbils sometimes resemble small prairie dogs. At this age their feet seem somewhat large for their body.

2. Gerbils as Pets

After earning the name "gentle gerbils" in the laboratory, it was almost inevitable that these animals should enter the pet world. By 1965, through TV appearances, press articles, classroom interest, and word-of-mouth, gerbils became well established as very desirable pets.

These are not "cuddly" pets, but they seem to enjoy being handled and will not bite unless they're mistreated. Their friendliness, curiosity, pert expressions, and jerky, squirrel-like movements are fascinating to adults and children alike.

Gerbils have simple requirements for housing, food, and water. They can be left unattended for days if food and water are available. They are clean, odorless, and easy to keep that way. They are healthy and hardy. They make very little noise.

Climate is no problem if temperature can be maintained within reasonable limits. There is no hibernation in winter or stupor in summer, and gerbils are active during the daytime. They have little tendency to escape and are relatively easy to recapture if they should get loose.

Because gerbils seem happiest and most active when kept in mated pairs, the question of what to do with their offspring must be considered. It seems likely that friends, neighbors, pet shops, and schools will be very accommodating in this respect, judging from the existing supply and demand conditions. An alternative might be to obtain a pair of gerbils beyond breeding age which still can provide you with plenty of interesting activity and friendly behavior.

The gerbil's overall attributes indicate that they will soon be a favorite pet in countless homes—city, farm, or suburban dwelling—as well as visitors to many school classrooms.

3.   Gerbil Behavior and Habits

Gerbils have several specific habits and customs which are interesting to observe. These are a part of the animals' daily life, and worthy of some knowledge by the pet owner so that he will understand his pets better. Certain behavior is not well understood and further study is needed to gain new knowledge about gerbils.

ACTIVITY CYCLE

The gerbil's life is one of cyclic activity. He alternates periods of intense activity with short periods of sleep or rest throughout the day. When awake, he darts to and fro like a chipmunk. He curiously investigates every new occurrence. He nibbles at food continually to support his bursts of energy. He burrows into his bedding, gnaws on available material, and makes nests. His intense participation in these activities makes it easy to understand why he needs occasional rest!

A gerbil often stretches out his forefeet and yawns almost like a cat or a dog. As you might guess, a nap soon follows. Sleep can be deep and uninterrupted; except for his breathing, you may wonder sometimes whether he is still alive. In warm weather, he may rearrange the bedding to lie on the bare cage floor. He'll curl up on his side, stretch out on his stomach, or even lie flat on his back! In cool weather, gerbils often sleep close together or on top of each other. They like to tuck their head down between their hind feet and curl their tail around their body—thus resembling a two-inch "ball of fluff."

During the gerbil's periods of rest or sleep, the pet owner should not disturb the animal. This would be contrary to the gerbil's natural way of life, and he might become irritable—like a child who misses his nap.

CURIOSITY

This trait dominates the gerbil's active behavior to a considerable extent. When you approach the gerbils' cage, they will invariably come to the nearest side to see what new food or plaything you have for them to try out. They're eager to inspect or investigate almost any toy or object offered to them—tubes, toy bridges or ladders, vehicles, baskets, carts, boxes, empty cans, pieces of cloth or paper, building blocks, etc. (Because of the gerbil's gnawing habits, be sure that these objects cannot harm the animals.) His interest is short-lived with one toy or new object, and curiosity makes him ready to explore a new one soon.

This curiosity drive is so great that a hungry gerbil subjected to a maze test with food at its end will stop to explore each "dead end" passage in the maze before he reaches the end!

If you stick your hand into his cage, the gerbil's first reaction is to sniff it and examine it further. Usually he'll want to climb your hand and arm for more exploring, if you are willing.

Fearlessness is closely related to curiosity at times. In captivity the gerbil has little chance to learn fear from his experience or his parents' experience. Sudden movements or noises may startle gerbils, especially the young ones, but this reaction seems to be one of surprise more than fear. Generally no fear is apparent on their exposure to strange objects, people, noises, lights, or animals. Because of this lack of fear, you should be cautious in allowing your gerbils to come into contact with other animals. Some dogs and cats can be trained to tolerate gerbils, but others may regard the gerbil as a tasty meal or a handy plaything to tease.

BURROWING

Burrowing and scratching are normal activities for gerbils. In the wild they spend much time burrowing to make their homes and to search for food among the desert scrub and grass. Their short forefeet make rapid digging motions, and the hind legs kick the excavated material to the rear—much like the lawn-digging actions of a dog. Sometimes the head is also used to push material or objects out of the way.

The sharp nails on the gerbil's forefeet can eventually burrow through cardboard or make scratches in wood or plastic. However, the author does not know of an instance where a pet owner has been scratched enough to break the skin.

On occasion you may look into the gerbil cage and think that you have lost a pet. Chances are that the "missing" animal has burrowed completely beneath the bedding material. Rap lightly on the cage and you'll probably see a cute, whiskery face pop up, like a miniature squirrel emerging from a pile of leaves!

GNAWING

The gerbil's incisors grow throughout his lifetime. If they're too long or too short, he could not survive long. In captivity this is seldom a problem—if necessary you can provide a block of wood for "tooth exercise," although the hard food in the diet usually suffices.

At one time or another, gerbils will attempt to gnaw or chew on almost any available material—bedding, nest material, paper, cardboard, cloth, wood, bone, plastic, and even metal. This is a normal part of their everyday life.

This litter of gerbils provides a wide variety of poses and expressions making it easy to understand why these animals are such fascinating pets.

A gerbil is a clean pet animal and his washing habits are similar to those of a cat. The tapered and tufted rump is typical of the male gerbil.

LOCOMOTION

The ability to jump with his hind limbs is a characteristic that makes the gerbil a unique pet and has earned him the nickname "pocket kangaroo." In the wild, gerbils can jump several feet if need be. Young gerbils can use their hind legs for jumping by the time they're weaned. When a cageful of youngsters is suddenly startled, they look like a box of jumping beans scattering in various directions! Older gerbils will not jump so frequently, although they still have the ability. In captivity, even unconfined gerbils seldom jump more than about 18 inches horizontally or 6 inches vertically.

Some gerbils hop straight up when startled. They can jump forward, backward, sideways, or even turn completely around in mid-air if they desire. The author has owned some which seemed to enjoy doing back-flips! To do this, they would leap toward the cage top, touch their nose and forepaws lightly against it to complete a loop, then land upright on their hind legs on the cage bedding.

Usually gerbils move about on all four feet, with their short forefeet providing limited balance and support. From time to time they pause to sit or stand on their hind legs like squirrels—this is their preferred eating or drinking

Gnawing is part of a gerbil's daily life. This collection of "sculptures" from different gerbils shows their carving ability in paper, plastic, wood and even metal.

position. To exercise their curiosity, gerbils will stand erect, stretch upward, and even lean backward slightly while still maintaining their balance.

The tail is used to good advantage. It gives the gerbil balance while sitting, standing, or on landing after a leap. During a jump, it may act like a rudder to help guide the animal through the air.

Gerbils can climb wire mesh vertically with no difficulty, but they cannot hang upside-down from a mesh cage roof for long, due to the particular structure of their legs and feet.

The young gerbil on the left is standing "on tiptoe" to observe something out of his line of vision. His playmate is more interested in shredding a piece of cloth.

A gerbil in sleeping position. The head is tucked down between the hind feet transforming the gerbil into a little ball of fluff.

NOISES

These pets are relatively quiet animals. Their only vocal sound is a faint, high-pitched *chee, chee,* more like the cheeping of a bird than the squeaking of a rodent. Even this sound is infrequent unless a litter of young is present or if the parents have a brief "family argument."

From weaning age, most gerbils can make a sound on the cage bedding or floor by rapidly drumming or thumping their hind legs. This staccato *ta-ta-TAT* may be a warning signal, like the slapping of a beaver's tail. It seems to signify **Attention!** and may be repeated by other gerbils within hearing. It also seems to indicate excitement in new surroundings or at mating time.

21

The rapid burrowing or scratching action of the forefeet against the cage floor or walls also produces a characteristic rustling or rasping sound.

GROOMING

Gerbils like to be clean, and they keep themselves well-groomed with little effort on your part.

Using forepaws and tongue, they "scrub" their face, head, ears, body, and tail in cat-like fashion. One gerbil will often groom another. These actions promote cleanliness, stimulate the skin, prevent matting of the fur, and help keep the coat glossy.

Because gerbils come from very dry climates, their skin produces certain natural oils to combat dryness. Dampness or high humidity may counteract the purpose of these oils and result in a ruffled coat, which the animals take care of by grooming and by rolling in dry bedding material.

4. Selecting Pet Gerbils

If you purchase your gerbils from a pet dealer or a reliable breeder, there should be no problem in assuring that your animals are healthy and from good stock.

To date there are no known mutations or color strains. However, it seems only a matter of time, statistics, and selective breeding before these occur, as was true with the hamster.

AGE AND SEX

Although the author's 10-year-old daughter has tamed "middle-aged" gerbils in a few days, it is more desirable to begin training with a younger animal. By age one month, the odds are that a gerbil will lead a full and healthy life; add a few weeks to this age just to increase your odds, and get your gerbils when they're about 6 to 8 weeks old. At this age they will be fairly rugged, not too nervous, and their appearance and actions will afford you much pleasure.

plastic, or glass are preferred for ease of cleaning. Wood is least expensive but also the least durable or sanitary. (Gerbils can and will gnaw exposed wood surfaces, unless flush, and they can scratch wood and plastic surfaces to some extent.)

Normally your gerbils will not jump high enough to escape from an aquarium or open-top cage, but it's best to provide some form of top or lid to keep out "intruders" and still allow ventilation. These covers can be made of wire mesh or be purchased in standard sizes from your pet dealer.

The spacing of the cage wire mesh or grid should be one-half inch or less; this will prevent sore spots from forming on the gerbil's nose during his attempts to gnaw the metal. Insect screening should not be used within the animals' reach, as they might scratch or gnaw through it.

Inexpensive plastic storage boxes fitted with a mesh top and a watering bottle can house weanling gerbils. Allow about 20 square inches of floor space per gerbil.

It is preferable that the cage sides and ends be solid to a height of several inches above the floor to reduce the scattering of the bedding material which may result from the animals' burrowing. This may also prevent the accidental loss of newborn gerbils through the mesh or grid openings, and it provides protection against drafts.

A ten gallon aquarium, even one that leaks, costs so little and makes such a safe and secure gerbil home, that this is the recommended abode for your gerbil pets. The watering bottle has been hung with a bent wire clothes hanger and the top has been made of mesh hardware cloth, but your petshop has snug screen covers for the top of the aquarium as well as lights.

BEDDING

Bedding material should be provided on the cage floor to a depth of 2 or 3 inches. The gerbils will arrange it to suit their needs, depending on the temperature and their own desires.

This material should be clean, absorbent, dustless, and non-toxic. Pine shavings, chips, coarse sawdust, excelsior, crushed corn cobs, husks, grass, leaves, or any commercial "litter" material will be adequate.

CLEANLINESS

Gerbils are perhaps the cleanest of all pet animals. Their body wastes amount to so little that the cage bedding material needs changing only every 2 or 3 weeks! And if a litter of young arrives at normal cage-cleaning time, you can wait until weaning time to change the bedding. Of course you should change the bedding if it becomes soaked due to spilled water or if it is obviously soiled. Bedding may have to be changed more frequently in warm weather than during cool weather.

Routine cage cleaning consists of a brief scraping and sweeping of the cage when the soiled bedding is removed. Several times a year you should use a household disinfectant solution to clean the cage and utensils (be sure to dry and air the cage thoroughly before returning the animals).

When your gerbils are put back in their cage after the bedding is renewed, they will burrow into it and work industriously to rearrange it. This is a good time to put a small piece of soft cloth in the cage for the gerbils to shred into nesting material which will last until the next bedding change.

If sufficient floor space is provided, gerbils are not afflicted with any kind of "paralysis." Even so, most gerbils will enjoy using a hamster exercise wheel, which provides a good outlet for their excess energy. Some gerbils may also like to use an inclined-disc exercise apparatus, which can be made rather easily.

A food container, a standard watering bottle, some toys or playthings, and a piece of wood for gnawing will complete the "furnishings" of the gerbils' home.

TEMPERATURE AND HUMIDITY

In his native environment the gerbil can stay comfortable by retreating to his burrow during the heat of the day or the chill of the night when necessary. In captivity his requirements are nearly the same as those of your home—about 70 to 80°F. and 40 to 60 percent relative humidity. Temperatures as low as 50°F. can be tolerated if sufficient bedding and nesting material are provided.

If your climate permits, gerbil cages can be located outdoors, assuming that you provide adequate protection against rain, sun, wind, and predators.

Gerbils kept in an aquarium or in transparent plastic cages must be protected from exposure to direct sunlight. The sun's rays, plus the insulating and possibly magnifying properties of the cage walls, might raise the inside temperature above 100°F., *which could be fatal*!

The cage can be kept in a basement, garage, or spare room, as desired. Because of the gerbil's cleanliness and lack of odor, there is usually no reason to prevent you from keeping them in almost any room of your household.

Several types of home-made breeding cages. These have wooden frameworks, hardboard sides and bottoms, wire mesh tops and ends. Each is 10 × 10 × 20 inches.

At the weaning age of three weeks, most gerbils have learned to eat solid foods. In this very large litter, all eight gerbils liked to sleep in a huddle in a jar lid, thus the ruffled coats.

your feeding routine. They do not hoard food and—*except for sunflower seeds*—they will not overeat.

Sunflower seeds are the gerbil's favorite treat. It is fascinating to watch a gerbil deftly hold and manipulate a seed in his forepaws, slit the shell with his sharp incisors, extract and devour the meat, then discard the husk and reach for another. This neat trick is mastered by most gerbils by age 3 weeks. These seeds should *not* form a large part of the diet, though, as they contain considerable fat, and your pets might develop a waistline problem!

Because gerbils are so clean and healthy you can put their food directly on the cage bedding. However, leftover food could become contaminated, and it is best to use a container. This can be a wire mesh or slotted metal food hopper, a small can, or a dish—preferably non-tippable. Be sure that the container has no sharp edges or openings that could injure or entrap a gerbil.

GREENS

Dry food should be supplemented with greens several times weekly to supply additional vitamins and minerals. You can offer fresh lettuce, celery, raw carrots or potatoes, kale, parsley, parsnips, apple peel, grass, dandelion, alfalfa, and similar foods in small amounts. This can be placed on the bedding. Gerbils normally will not eat any contaminated food, but you should remove the leftover portion daily.

Your pets are not so susceptible to diarrhea as some small rodents. Nevertheless, greens should be given only in limited quantities to avoid the risk of intestinal disorders.

Within the limitations discussed, the gerbil's diet allows you considerable possibilities for variation. Individual animals may show certain food preferences, and you'll enjoy testing their tastes from time to time.

Greens should only be offered in limited quantities. Discourage young children from randomly feeding your pet gerbils.

The only food a gerbil will overeat is sunflower seed. Gerbils, and most other rodents and seed-eating birds, enjoy sunflower seeds to such an extent that they have become a popular enough pet food for almost every petshop to carry in large enough quantities to meet customer demand.

Although gerbils need little drinking water, they readily learn to drink from a standard watering bottle.

DRINKING WATER

The gerbil's desert heritage means that his drinking water demands are slight. In fact, if you feed sufficient greens, a separate source of water is not necessary! However, your pets will readily accept drinking water if available, and it is generally desirable and convenient that you do provide a supply of fresh water.

Dishes or pans are not satisfactory. The burrowing actions of the animals will upset or contaminate the water. Young gerbils might drown in the container. Gerbils prefer to drink from a "sitting" position.

A standard hamster watering bottle costs little, is easily attached to the cage with a spring or wire clip, and it seldom needs refilling. Either a glass or a metal spout can be used. Since gerbils can gnaw the metal kind, occasionally you'll have to file the tip smooth. To provide a convenient drinking height, and to prevent the bedding from acting as a wick to drain the bottle, you should locate the bottle so that the end of the spout is several inches above the top of the cage bedding.

If your gerbil cage is an aquarium or other solid-walled container, you can easily bend a length of wire to support the inverted watering bottle inside one corner of the cage.

VACATION TIME

Gerbils travel well, but most likely you'll decide to leave them at home when you go on a vacation. You can leave these pets unattended for as long as a week because of their limited demands.

Before you depart, provide fresh bedding, an accessible container holding plenty of dry food, and a watering bottle of fresh water (make sure it doesn't leak). Give each gerbil a good-sized chunk of raw carrot and potato—this will supplement their dry diet and provide an "emergency" water supply. Double-check to see that the cage is escape-proof and located where direct sunlight and temperature extremes or drafts will be avoided.

If your vacation lasts more than a week, of course you must arrange to have someone replenish the animals' food and water at least weekly and change the bedding every 2 or 3 weeks.

Children and gerbils go well together. The author's son handles untamed gerbils without fear by either party.

Even girls like gerbils!

7. Handling and Training Gerbils

When you first receive your gerbils, you can offer them food and water, but it's desirable to let them rest for a day before they're handled. This will give them some time to recover from any transportation involved and allow them to become somewhat accustomed to their new home.

HANDLING METHODS

The preferred method of picking up a gerbil is to place one or both hands, cupped with palm up, underneath his body so as to lift him up. At first, let him walk onto your open palm before picking him up; this will prepare him for the experience. Later you can lift him with a gentle but fairly rapid "scooping" motion with one or both hands. Don't grasp his middle—he may feel trapped and struggle to escape. An alternate method is to lift him by his tail, which should be held near its base to prevent injury.

Once a gerbil is lifted a few inches above any solid surface, he has a good sense of height and will seldom jump or climb down without considerable deliberation.

Even an older, untamed gerbil can be easily and safely coaxed to accept his favorite food (sunflower seeds) from your fingertips.

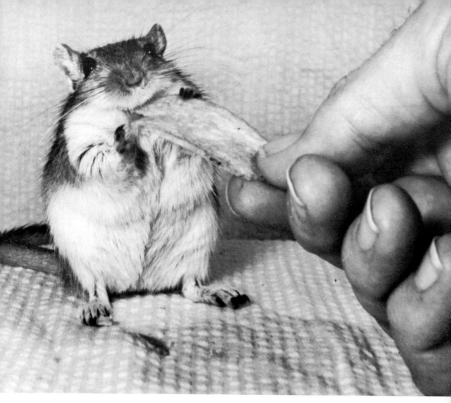

Food is an important reward during taming and training. This gerbil seems fat and jovial in the photo; he's just bitten off a piece of corn chip.

If you lift your pets to any height, it's a good policy to hold them in the palm of one hand and hold the base of their tail with the other hand to avoid accidental falls. When gerbils are allowed to exercise on a tabletop, they recognize that they should not venture beyond the edge, but in some exuberant moment they might skid off it or simply forget that it's there, and you must be alert to prevent such accidents.

Your pets will enjoy climbing up your arm or your clothes, and they can perch on your shoulder (don't make any abrupt movements that could result in a fall). They like to crawl in and out of collars, pockets, or hoods; be sure that they don't burrow or chew so as to damage your clothing on these occasions.

43

Gerbils make excellent pets for children (and adults) of all ages. Learn how to handle your pet gerbil carefully without squeezing or frightening the animal.

The author's family has handled thousands of gerbils yet never has any one of them received a gerbil bite severe enough to break the skin.

The author's daughter is watching with anticipation, wondering where the gerbil will pop up next in the jumper pocket.

Training and play sessions can be fun for your gerbils if you allow them to discover some "treasures" of sunflower seeds.

TAMING AND TRAINING

In thousands of handlings of many different and untamed gerbils of all ages and under varying conditions, the author has never been bitten so that a break in the skin resulted. Several gerbil breeders report similar experiences. Generally a gerbil will bite with force only if he is handled improperly —by chasing, teasing, squeezing, etc. Of course if you place your finger directly in front of his mouth and hold it there, you *may* receive a slight nip if the animal is hungry or if he's gnawing on some object—this reaction is almost instinctive. If a bite results in broken skin, you should apply appropriate medication and ensure that you are protected against tetanus, as with any animal bite. (Note: The U.S. Public Health Service informed the author that

Gerbils are inquisitive,
clean, tame, safe pets
for children. They are
about the same size as a
small toy and have
been found to be
absolutely enchanting
to all who observe them.

When you first obtain your pet gerbil, he will weigh little more than a letter. This one is washing his face while being weighed in.

it has no specific statistics concerning rabies among gerbils and hamsters, and referred to the World Health Organization's Expert Committee on Rabies, whose report states that no evidence of this disease was found during surveys of small wild rodents.)

The gerbil's gentleness when handled, his curiosity, friendliness, activity cycle, and food preferences are your clues toward successful taming and training. Also his intelligence seems high for his size—for example, he learns to avoid certain situations or conditions about 10 times faster than white rats.

Patience, understanding, repetition, and reward are essential in taming and training. They are your tools for developing in your pets a sense of trust and confidence.

Training sessions should be brief, especially with young gerbils, who may be jumpy and nervous-acting for a few weeks. Keep in mind the gerbil's activity cycle—if you interrupt or prevent a needed rest period, they may become somewhat irritable.

Be slow, calm, but deliberate in your movements and voice. Let the gerbils become accustomed to your relative size; even your hand may seem like a giant to them!

At feeding time, let the animals eat some seeds or bits of lettuce from your fingers. While they're eating, gently scratch their head, ears, or back with your finger; this will help accustom them to your touch. Later, during training

Gerbils quickly learn to play follow-the-leader. Here they are exploring a home-made tunnel made from paper tubes which are a by-product of most kitchen tissues.

A normal, healthy, active gerbil.

sessions, offer various treats as a reward, especially if you're attempting to teach some simple tricks.

As you progress, let your gerbils out of the cage so that they can have some freedom in a limited area such as a large box, a table top, or even a bathtub. Gerbils will enjoy these "outings" periodically, especially if you provide some interesting objects to explore. Probably the gerbils will

Children's toys can easily become gerbil's playthings. Here the author's family is putting on a gerbil circus.

return to their cage voluntarily for food or rest; otherwise you can easily coax them to return or else pick them up.

You may enjoy staging a gerbil "circus." All you need is a large box, two or more gerbils, some toys and objects that gerbils appreciate, and an appreciative audience. Almost any cardboard or wood box will do, or you can use a metal tub, a plastic sand box, or a rigid wading pool.

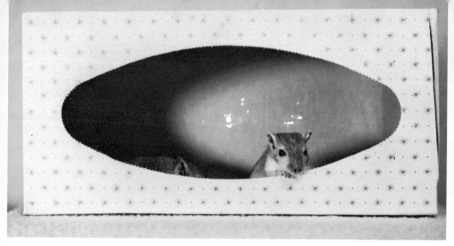

An empty box makes an interesting "second home" for gerbils to play in or chew on.

Gerbils should not be allowed the run of your household. Eventually they might get lost or injured. However, you might give them the freedom of one room or an enclosed porch occasionally; make sure that the space is sealed off to keep gerbils in and dogs or cats out. You will have to watch your step—literally—because gerbils often come near your feet, either out of curiosity or due to some need for physical security.

Your gerbils can be taken outdoors, weather permitting, but they should be confined to some box, fencing, or other enclosure. If they escape from your control, they could be victims of domestic animals or birds, predators, poisonous sprays, or winter weather.

8. Breeding Gerbils

In captivity gerbils breed best in mated pairs (it's not known whether they follow this monogamous pattern in the wild). Two or more females kept with a single male will result in failure or disaster: either there will be no productive matings or the females may bully the male to death. On losing a mate, a female gerbil is reluctant to receive a new one, and may completely refuse to accept him.

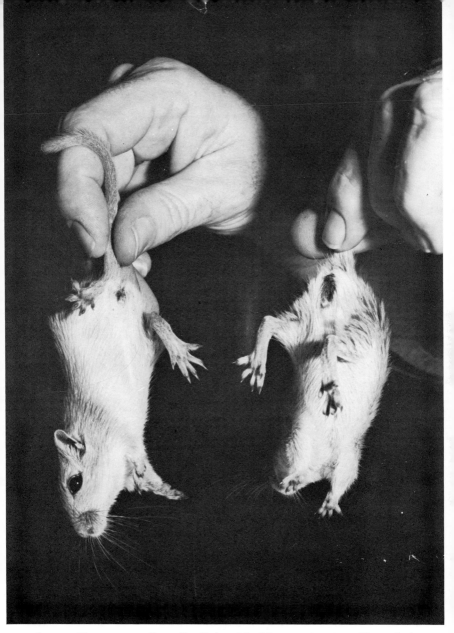

Sex markings are usually easily distinguished by weaning time. The male is on the right. If you pick up a gerbil by his tail, hold it as close to the base as possible.

Some gerbils love to play in a hamster-type exercise wheel.

MATURITY AND REPRODUCTION

Sexual maturity occurs at age 9 to 12 weeks. Generally the sexes can be distinguished by 3 weeks. The male's body has a tapered bulge—usually tufted—near the base of his tail, and there is a dark-colored scrotal pouch. The female's rump is more rounded; the genital opening is close to the anal opening. As a rule, mature males are somewhat larger in size and weight than females.

The initial pairing of gerbils nearly always results in compatibility if the pairing is accomplished at or slightly

These photos illustrate the type of home-made toys which gerbils enjoy.

before maturity. When you buy gerbils from a pet dealer, this detail may already have been taken care of; if not, you'll know in a day or two whether a "happy marriage" will result. Once the pair is thus established, the male can usually be left safely with the female at all times including the nursing of a litter.

If desired, you can provide a wood or metal nesting box, about 6 inches on a side with a suitable doorway, but most gerbils seem content with nests built from cloth, paper, or leaves, which they shred into strips with their teeth and forepaws. Both the male and the female participate in this project.

Your pets can breed throughout the year; there is no apparent seasonal variation. The breeding (heat) cycle has not been determined, but it may be short—perhaps every 4 to 10 days. The female probably goes into heat in the afternoon and is out of it by morning. Mating often occurs immediately after the arrival of a litter, and sometimes

Gerbils often make a bird-like nest from a piece of cloth which they chew and tear into shreds. This mother is giving a bath to one of her youngsters.

Usually it is safe to leave the male and female together at all times. The male often "sits on the nest" and may develop what appears to be affection for his offspring.

during the nursing period. The gestation period is about 24 days.

Unless you're a careful observer, you may not be able to detect a pregnancy without weighing the female. Because gerbils are naturally so quiet, the first indication of a new litter may be the high-pitched calls of the newborn animals. Most litters are born during the night or early morning, however the writer has witnessed some births in mid-afternoon. Birth is relatively uncomplicated and painless, requiring only an hour or so even for a large litter; since there is no help needed on your part, it's advisable that you simply leave the female undisturbed at this time.

The litter size ranges from 1 to 10, with an average of 4 or 5 young; the ratio of males to females is nearly 1 to 1. The majority of females will bear their first litter by age 6 months. About one-third of all females may have their first litter at age 3 to 4 months.

One-day-old gerbils. They are born furless, deaf, blind and toothless.

The female's reproductive life may last to age 20 months, although it usually ceases by age 14 months. During this period as many as 10 litters can be produced; the average is 6 or 7, however. Considering these figures and a survival rate of about 75%, you can expect the average female to rear about 20 young in her lifetime, which partly explains the relatively high cost of your pets. It seems likely that future improvements in nutrition, care, and genetic selection of breeding stock will result in a somewhat higher reproduction rate.

SUCCESSFUL BREEDING "SECRETS"

As a pet owner, you may not be able to duplicate some of the favorable conditions achieved by commercial breeders of gerbils. Nevertheless, if you follow the suggestions given below, you should have an excellent chance of success in breeding your gerbils:

(1) Ensure that sufficient cage space, bedding, and nesting material are provided.

(2) Keep your gerbils' diet relatively high in protein and low in fat.

(3) **Provide adequate privacy. A cage with one or more opaque sides may help.**

(4) **Locate the cage where there is a minimum of disturbance from household noise and traffic.**

(5) **Avoid unnecessary handling of gerbils in the evening.**

YOUNG GERBILS

Newborn gerbils are naked and pink, blind, toothless, and deaf. They are little more than an inch long and weigh a tenth of an ounce. The percentage of live births is rather high and cannibalism is rare. If the female should eat her young, it may be that they died from a lack of milk due to some dietary deficiency; you may be able to prevent this by giving the female some evaporated milk during pregnancy and nursing.

The male can be left with the female and the litter although his "duties" usually consist only of occasional shepherding the young back to their nest and sitting on the nest to help keep the young warm.

Shortly after weaning, at three weeks of age. The ruffled coat on one of the gerbils is due to his just having emerged from a "pile" of sleeping gerbils. The coat will slick down in a few minutes.

The first week of life is critical. Handling the animals during this period is not recommended—such disturbances might cause the mother to trample, smother, or desert her young unintentionally.

Some females fail to raise a small litter successfully, yet their next litter may be a large one in which all young survive. These inconsistencies may be due to dietary factors which are still in need of study.

When the young stray from their nest—which can happen at an early age—the mother usually returns them by scooping them with her forefeet, pushing them with her nose, or even by picking them up bodily in her mouth (these measures do not seem to cause any harm, however). Then she'll busily re-shape the nest to keep all her babies warm and secure. If the litter is large, some females will keep their young in two nests, dividing the nursing time about equally.

Although you can offer some bits of bread crusts soaked in milk, this is not a necessity for a nursing mother if you feed a balanced diet and make drinking water available.

By age 3 days the young have some dark pigmentation and they can crawl in an ungainly manner. At 5 or 6 days an undercoat of seal-gray hair is visible and the ears are open. By 2 weeks the fur is reddish-brown; the animals now look something like miniature fawn-colored boxer puppies (some persons refer to young gerbils as "pups"). In a few more days most gerbils have incisors for their first gnawing attempts, their eyelids begin to separate, and their activity is generally more coordinated.

At age 3 weeks gerbils weigh about one-half ounce. They can now eat solid food, drink from a watering bottle, climb wire mesh, stand up, jump, and thump their hind legs. Though tiny, they are truly gerbils and they should be weaned now. This may seem to be a tender age for weaning, but the animals adjust easily and it is important to remove them from their parents to avoid the space and parental care problems if another litter should arrive in a few days (this is the exception—not the rule).

Weanlings may be sexed and placed in separate cages or kept in a community group until they are about 8 weeks of age, when they should be separated to prevent inbreeding. In pairing gerbils, it is a good policy to keep their relationship no closer than second cousin.

The young can be housed in smaller quarters than adults, but you should allow about 20 square inches per animal.

For the first week after weaning, you may want to put some unsweetened breakfast cereal in with the gerbils' regular solid food; this is easily handled and the animals seem to like it. Some milk-soaked bread crusts may be offered also, if desired. The use of a watering bottle is quickly learned if the spout is located so that the young can reach it.

Some litters may have one or two runts, due to nursing difficulties or dietary deficiencies. Often these gerbils will grow to normal size and catch up with others of their litter. If the runts are bullied by their brothers and sisters, you can isolate the runts to permit an opportunity for more unhindered development.

9. Your Gerbils' Health

Gerbils are relatively healthy and hardy and will remain so with a minimum of care from their owner. You can expect their normal life span to be 3 to 4 years.

Preventative measures are important because the successful treatment of some diseases of small animals is difficult to impossible. These measures would include proper diet, fresh water, reasonable cleanliness, sufficient cage space and ventilation, and protection against dampness and extreme temperatures or drafts.

Diarrhea or intestinal disorders seem to be rare among gerbils. If such illnesses occur, they could be related to the diet—perhaps too many leafy greens, or the presence of contaminated food. In those instances you should modify the diet, change the bedding, and isolate the sick animal.

Colds and similar viruses are seldom a problem but their symptoms would be listless activity or droopiness, runny eyes or nose, or lack of appetite. Isolation is necessary, and sick animals should be protected against drafts, low temperatures, or dampness. In winter you can give vitamin drops or codliver oil from a dropper or by placing it on some solid food.

Balding, accompanied by an off-color coat, occurs in young gerbils occasionally. If these animals survive beyond weaning age, they usually develop normally. The cause of this ailment is not known; it may stem from a dietary deficiency.

A *"hypnotic" condition* is sometimes observed when a gerbil is handled. The affected animal "freezes" with his forefeet extended stiffly, and his body may tremble slightly; after a few minutes, normal activity is resumed and there is no after-effect apparent. This condition is believed to result from a vitamin B deficiency and you may be able to correct it by feeding more cereals, grains, or other foods rich in vitamin B.

Eye injuries or infections can result from active playing, fighting, or running into sharp obstacles. Treatment may consist of bathing the eye with warm water, rinsing with a fresh 10% solution of argyrol, or applying an antibiotic eye ointment. Some "old" gerbils are subject to an eye condition which causes exaggerated bulging of the eye, inflammation, and protrusion of the "third eyelid." The cause and cure are not known.

Body sores or injuries, if minor, can be treated with a safe, mild antiseptic; don't attempt to bandage. Ulcerations of the mouth and nose—perhaps from vigorous burrowing actions —also respond to similar treatment.

External parasites (fleas, mites, lice) should be suspected if your gerbils scratch excessively or bite their fur frequently. Apply a dusting powder or a spray which is considered safe for use on cats or hamsters.

Consult a veterinarian for his care of any illnesses or conditions obviously beyond household assistance.